RACHEL
The Story of Rachel Carson

AMY EHRLICH

ILLUSTRATED BY WENDELL MINOR

Voyager Books • Harcourt, Inc.

ORLANDO   AUSTIN   NEW YORK
SAN DIEGO   LONDON

www.HarcourtBooks.com

First Voyager Books edition 2008

Voyager Books is a trademark of Harcourt, Inc., registered in the United States of America and/or other jurisdictions.

The Library of Congress has cataloged the hardcover edition as follows:
Ehrlich, Amy, 1942–
Rachel: the story of Rachel Carson/written by Amy Ehrlich; illustrated by Wendell Minor.
p. cm.
1. Carson, Rachel, 1907–1964—Juvenile literature.   2. Biologists—United States—Biography—Juvenile literature.   3. Environmentalists—United States—Biography—Juvenile literature.   [1. Carson, Rachel, 1907–1964.   2. Biologists.   3. Environmentalists.   4. Women—Biography.]
I. Minor, Wendell, ill. II. Title. QH31.C33E47 2003 570'.92—dc21 00-13115
ISBN 978-0-15-216227-6
ISBN 978-0-15-206324-5 pb

A C E G H F D B

The illustrations in this book were done in watercolor and gouache on Strathmore 500 Bristol.
The display type was set in Pouty.
The text type was set in Centaur.
Color separations by Bright Arts Ltd., Hong Kong
Manufactured by South China Printing Company, Ltd., China
Production supervision by Christine Witnik
Designed by Wendell Minor and Judythe Sieck

For Airie Lindsay. And in memory of Mary Bunting Smith.—A. E.

For children of all ages who discover a sense of wonder in nature.—W. M.

The Rachel Carson National Wildlife Refuge comprises more than
five thousand acres along the Maine seashore. For more information, visit:
www.fws.gov/northeast/rachelcarson

The author and the artist gratefully acknowledge the assistance of the Rachel Carson Council, Inc.,
in the making of this book. Formed in 1965 to carry on her work, the council responds to questions
from the public on pesticide dangers and publishes scientific information about the environment.
For more information, visit:
www.rachelcarsoncouncil.com

The author gratefully acknowledges the help of the Rainy Lake Writers and the Oberholtzer Foundation.

Bibliography

Brooks, Paul. *The House of Life: Rachel Carson at Work.* Boston: Houghton Mifflin Company, 1972.

Carson, Rachel. *Under the Sea-Wind: A Naturalist's Picture of Ocean Life.* New York: Oxford University Press, 1941.

———. *The Sea Around Us.* New York: Oxford University Press, 1951.

———. *The Edge of the Sea.* Boston: Houghton Mifflin Company, 1955.

———. *Silent Spring.* Boston: Houghton Mifflin Company, 1962.

———. *The Sense of Wonder.* New York: Harper & Row, 1965.

Freeman, Martha. *Always, Rachel: The Letters of Rachel Carson and Dorothy Freeman.* Boston: Beacon Press, 1995.

Lear, Linda. *Rachel Carson: Witness for Nature.* New York: Henry Holt and Company, 1997.

The Sea Fossil

1912

Rachel's house was far from the ocean, hundreds of miles inland at a bend on the Allegheny River in Pennsylvania. There were no seagulls there, no sharks or whales. But one day she found a fossil, a single dark spiral lodged in a rock at her feet. She brought it to show her mother, and they looked it up in a book. The fossil was a sea creature, her mother said. Millions of years ago the ocean had covered their land and left it behind.

Imagine! Beyond the fields and orchards, beyond the woods where she played with her dogs, beyond the Allegheny and the town of Springdale and the city of Pittsburgh, there was a vast ocean even now. At night Rachel lay in bed, her thoughts turning like waves.

A Silver Badge

1918

Rachel's dearest friend was her mother. They walked outdoors each afternoon, naming the insects and birds and plants, and they read books and studied nature together. Rachel was the youngest child in the family, solitary and odd and bright. Her mother let her know that she was different from Robert and Marian. More was expected of her.

Every month Rachel waited for *St. Nicholas Magazine* to come in the mail. The best part was the stories that children wrote themselves. You could win gold and silver badges if your story was chosen. She decided to send one in. It was called "A Battle in the Clouds," about an air fight in the war.

One month passed, then two, three, four, five. Finally, here came *St. Nicholas* again, and "A Battle in the Clouds" was printed in it, winner of a silver badge.

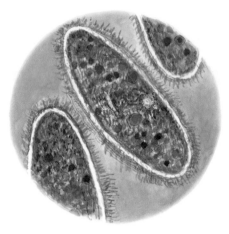

Under a Microscope

1927

Rachel was in biology class. Even though she was planning to be a writer, all the students at Pennsylvania College for Women had to take science. The teacher, Miss Skinker, helped her focus her slide. A transparent, elongated paramecium drifted slowly across the microscope's field. To Rachel its shape held the pattern of raindrops sliding down her window, and sandbars in the Allegheny, and clouds in the sky. In that simple one-celled organism she saw the complexity of the universe.

The next time her mother came to visit, Rachel said she was changing her major to biology. She'd always loved nature, but now she'd be able to learn what lay beneath its surface.

Woods Hole

1929

*T*he Woods Hole Marine Biology Laboratory on Cape Cod was surrounded by ocean, and it was all that Rachel had dreamed of. She sat at the same lab tables as famous university biologists, men and women both, and could work on her own research project, studying a nerve in the turtle's brain.

Her friend Mary Frye from college was at Woods Hole, too. Mary and Rachel liked to walk by the ocean when the tide was low. The currents of the water crossed over each other in rippled lines, like the tide lines edged with seaweed on the beach. And when the tide was coming in, there was a great *whoosh* of water and the earlier lines were erased. Rachel watched the sea with a writer's eyes and then went back to the Woods Hole research library to find out why it ebbs and flows.

Hawk Mountain

1945

Money was scarce in the Carson family. Rachel's father had never been able to hold a job for long, and Marian and Robert had moved back home, Marian with two children now. The only one who could support them all was Rachel. She got a job editing documents at the U.S. Bureau of Fisheries, a woman ashore, hardly even a scientist.

Wherever she went, Rachel carried a small spiral notebook to make notes on what she saw. She had it with her one weekend, birding on Hawk Mountain. Mists were drifting over the valley and hawks rode the wind, sailing on an ocean of air.

Rachel thought that if she could earn money from her nature writing, it might add space and distance to her own cramped life.

The Sea Around Us

1951

*I*n the books she wrote, Rachel explored the ocean. On its sunlit surface, microscopic plankton grazed on pastures of microscopic plants called diatoms, trillions of both in the water you could scoop up in your hands. Shoals of fish hunted one another farther down— herring and anchovy and mackerel, and the great white shark and the blue whale. And hundreds of fathoms deep, swimming in the inky darkness of drowned canyons and mountain ranges, were fish whose bodies glowed luminously so they could find their prey.

Rachel's readers liked roaming the ocean's great spaces. Now when they stood on a beach looking at the sea, which curved at the horizon with the earth's curve, they saw that it was full of mystery and beauty, teeming with life.

Collecting Specimens

1953

Rachel had a summer cottage built in Maine along the estuary of the Sheepscot River, near a place called Dogfish Head. A steep stairway led over the kelp-covered rocks to the shore. Up and down she went on it, carrying specimens to study with her microscope. Gray sea squirts, pale pink hydroids, a tiny starfish, a patch of green sponge—flowers that were not plants but animals, delicately moving, searching for food.

The best time for collecting was on the spring tides of the new moon. Rachel's guests to the cottage came, too, and looked under the microscope. But it was Rachel alone who, with her dungarees rolled up, went back to return the living creatures to their home.

Phosphorescence

1956

*O*n a windy night in August when the tide was high, Rachel and her niece Marjie went down to the sea to tie up a raft. In the surf were sheets of phosphorescence, sparkles of green and silver swirling and falling on the sand. Then Rachel and Marjie noticed a single light flying on its own into the water. A firefly had been lost and was trying to join the others. They saved it from drowning just in time.

This was a story Rachel loved for the communication that it showed between different species. She wanted to put it in a book for children. But Marjie died a year later, and Rachel was left to bring up Marjie's son, Roger, who was only five. For a long time she felt helpless, as lost as the firefly.

The Lost Woods

1957

*T*he woods near Rachel's cottage were shadowed with spruce trees, but in the open patches, reindeer moss grew and the pines smelled sweet in the sunshine. If you were lucky, you could sometimes hear the silvery song of a hermit thrush.

Rachel and her summer friend Dorothy Freeman loved these woods for their stillness and peace. But one day they saw that the road out to Dogfish Head was being widened by the town. There was a land boom in Maine, and they worried that the few wild places remaining on the seashore would soon be gone. Rachel knew that people, as well as other creatures, needed the sanctuary of wildness. She tried to buy the woods as a nature preserve, but the owners wouldn't sell. They wanted to get a better price.

Listening

1958

Rachel knew how to listen. When she got a letter from Mrs. Olga Owens Huckins saying that all the songbirds on her land died after airplanes had sprayed poisons to kill mosquitoes, she wrote to entomologists and ornithologists to find out why. They told a terrible story. Birds and grasshoppers, butterflies and bees, and fish in the rivers were all being killed. The poisons were everywhere—on the grasses that cows ate, and in their milk and meat, and in our own bodies, too.

Rachel, who loved the world so much, was frightened and angry. How could people cause it such harm? Didn't they see that everything was connected in an intricate web of life?

Silent Spring

1962

*I*t took Rachel four years to write a book about the dangers she'd discovered. She called it *Silent Spring* because if the birds were killed, their songs would not be heard in springtime. When the book came out, the companies that made the poisons attacked it. And they attacked Rachel, too. She was only a woman, after all, emotional and unreliable.

But other people believed her. They argued back and forth in the newspapers, on television, and in Washington. Committees were formed in Congress to investigate the poisons. Rachel dealt with both sides calmly, knowing she'd done all that she could. She was like a tiny, nearly transparent ghost crab she'd once written about, alone on a beach at night, facing the roaring surf.

A Migration of Butterflies

1963

Rachel needed her courage for something else, too, something more private and lonely. She was fighting for her own life against cancer.

One afternoon in September, when the Maine sky was dark blue and the goldenrod was blooming, Rachel and Dorothy Freeman went to Newagen Point and watched a migration of monarch butterflies. They drifted by, one by one and then more and more, their fragile wings like stained glass. The monarchs were flying to Mexico. Only a few would return.

Later on Rachel told her friend not to be sad. She said that just as the butterflies had their own cycle of life, so did each human being. Her time was nearing its end, but the rhythms of nature would go on. Spring would follow winter. Fish still swam in the ocean and the birds were singing.

Epilogue

Rachel Carson died on April 14, 1964. The pesticides report of the President's Science Advisory Committee confirmed the toxic effects of DDT and the other poisons she'd described, as did two Senate committee hearings on environmental hazards. It is generally agreed that today's environmental movement began with the publication of *Silent Spring.*

Although she was unable to buy her beloved Lost Woods, a seventy-eight-acre Maine wildlife refuge was named in her honor in 1970. The Rachel Carson Salt Pond Preserve has woodland, overgrown meadows, and coastline on Muscongus Bay near Pemaquid Point. At low tide there is a large pool where you can see many of the sea plants and creatures that Rachel Carson studied and loved.